MODERN MAPS

By Julie Haydon

Contents

How a Map is Made

A map is a drawing of the surface of the Earth or some other body in space, such as the Moon. A map can show a small area or a large area. Different types of maps show different features.

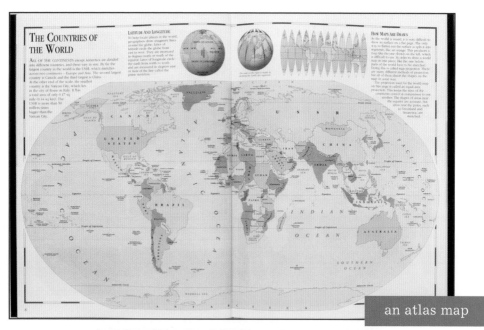

an atlas map

This topographic map shows how high or low the land is.

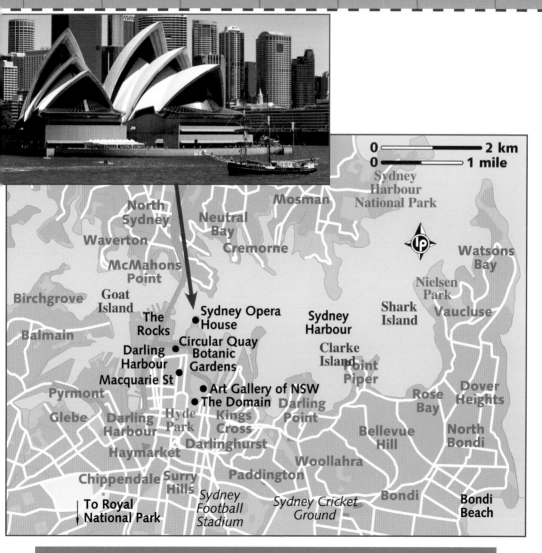

a map showing the location of the Sydney Opera House, Australia

Most maps are flat and show a bird's-eye view of an area. This means they show only the length and width of the features on the map and not their height.

Many maps help people find places and plan trips.

Map making is called cartography. People who make maps are called cartographers.

a cartographer at work

First, a cartographer gets information about the area that is to be mapped. Sometimes the information already exists in other forms, such as other maps. New information can come from surveying the land, and from machines such as cameras on board satellites and aeroplanes.

an aerial photograph of New York City, USA

a satellite map of New York City, USA

Then the cartographer plans the map. Decisions are made about the design of the map, including which symbols, colours, words, lines and grids to use. A key, or legend, is included on the map to explain what these design elements mean.

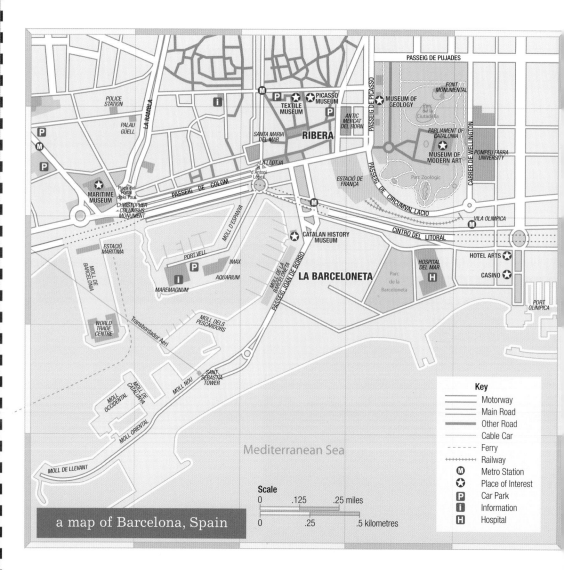

a map of Barcelona, Spain

Mediterranean Sea

Scale

| 0 | .125 | .25 miles |
| 0 | .25 | .5 kilometres |

Key

———	Motorway
———	Main Road
———	Other Road
———	Cable Car
- - - -	Ferry
+++++++	Railway
Ⓜ	Metro Station
✪	Place of Interest
🅿	Car Park
ⓘ	Information
🅷	Hospital

Vielha

FRANCE

ANDORRA

La Seu
d'Urgell

Figueres

CATALONIA

Vic

Girona

Balaguer

Manresa

Lleida

Tàrrega

Terrassa

Granollers

Sabadell

Vilafranca
del Penedès

Badalona

Barcelona

Barcelona-Prat

Reus

Tarragona

Mediterranean Sea

Tortosa

Scale
0   20   40 miles

0   20   40 kilometres

FRANCE

ANDORRA

CATALONIA

Barcelona

SPAIN

a map of Catalonia, Spain

The cartographer must also decide on the map's scale. An area on a map is always shown much smaller than it really is. However, the features must be the correct size and the correct distance apart when compared to each other. This is called drawing to scale. The scale is shown on the map.

Next, the cartographer draws the map on a computer. Once the map has been checked for errors, it is printed on paper and sent to shops, or it is made available electronically.

Finally, people use the map to get information about that area.

Maps are carefully planned and designed to make sure the information is correct.

This map has been downloaded onto a handheld device.

Paper or Electronic Maps?

Up until the last thirty years, people who wanted a portable map had to use one that had been printed on paper.

viewing a map on a mobile phone

Today, technology makes it possible for people to use maps that can be read on machines such as computers and mobile phones.

So which is better – a paper map or an electronic map?

11

Paper maps are useful. They are usually cheap to buy and easy to store. People who do not like using technology may find them easier to use than electronic maps. Paper maps can be read without any extra equipment.

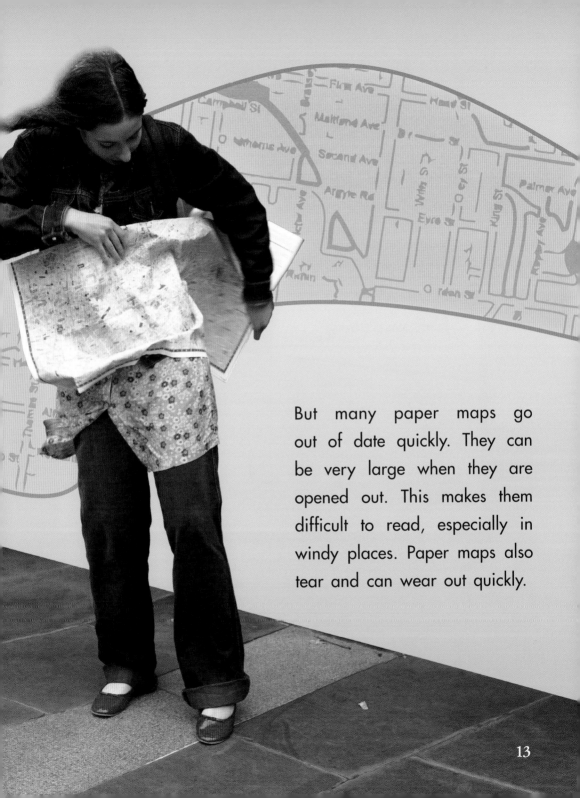

But many paper maps go out of date quickly. They can be very large when they are opened out. This makes them difficult to read, especially in windy places. Paper maps also tear and can wear out quickly.

Electronic maps have their advantages. They can be easily uploaded onto devices that often have many helpful features, such as the ability to zoom in. Some electronic devices have features that show people the fastest or shortest way from one place to another. They can even tell how long the journey should take.

a GPS navigation system in a car

Still, electronic maps need electronic equipment to make them work. Sometimes, this equipment is expensive and it can be difficult to use. This kind of equipment also needs a battery or electricity supply. Electronic equipment, such as a mobile phone, is no longer portable when it is charging.

Both paper maps and electronic maps have advantages and disadvantages. However, as technology improves and people become more comfortable with the idea of electronic maps, fewer paper maps will be sold. It seems likely that electronic maps will become more popular in the future.